<u>NO INJECTIONS NEEDED</u>

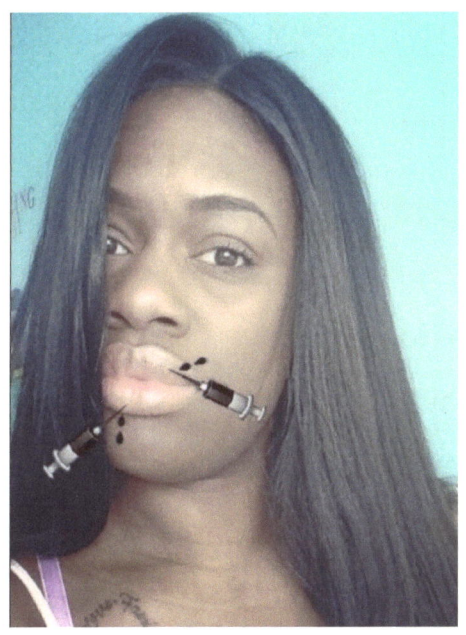

THANK YOU

Dear Beverly,

You have so many beautiful features, passed down to me from generation to generation. The love I have for you I can not put it into words. As a completed project on my entrepreneurial journey this book is dedicated to you. This is a project that is authentic and it comes directly from my heart. There were many projects I've started but didn't finish and some I am still in the process of completing. When things got hard for me you cheered me on anyway. I couldn't be happier and I am forever grateful to call you my mom. You've been there through every single struggle I've ever encountered in my life. Thank you, for these beautiful full lips you have given me genetically. Although, this is not my life's memoir this is just a few of my experiences with having full lips.

I Love You Mom

Elementary School

I remember my first day of school, I was so excited to meet my new teacher and make some new friends. The year I started school I wasn't starting pre-k, I was going straight to first grade. I had over extended my stay in upper Manhattan daycare. I was one smart cookie by the time it was ready for me to go to school. My entry test scores allowed me to qualify for a first grade class. I remember it like it was yesterday, I was wearing a blue dress with white stockings. It was so chilly that day but you couldn't tell me I wasn't cute. My mom did my hair in two pony tails and made sure my clothes were ironed neatly. My teacher's name was Ms. Canlas, a very tall slim woman. She was such a sweet lady. I could always remember her saying "Put your thinking cap on Aquira", whenever I felt like something was just to hard to solve. I would put on my imaginary thinking cap and just like that it worked, I would get almost every question right. Today I still put on that cap when life seems to be a little bit hard, the only difference is I mediate instead of thinking and the answers flow to me. That first grade year, I was so eager to make as many friends as possible. Everybody I came across just had to know about my twin cats named Chris and Cross. My siblings and I named them after the rap group that was hot around that time. We used to dance in my mother's living room to their songs all the time. My mother dropped me off to school that morning with a sense of urgency, only because she was rushing to get to work and she didn't want to be late. When she dropped me off she made sure she mentioned to me in her very stern voice.

"Make sure that you are good today, listen to your teachers, and pay attention. NO talking Aquira."

She meant it and I knew by the tone of her voice she was serious. I was always so talkative, and that would always keep me in trouble. However, there was something that my mother didn't warn me about. Something that followed me all the way to my adult years. What my mom didn't tell me was that the little boys and girls in my class would make fun of my LIPS. I don't know why she never mention something like this to me. Besides, my mom and I have the same exact lips. I thought to myself, maybe she didn't go through the same things as I did or maybe she wanted me to be as positive as possible about my first day and not mention anything at all. Maybe it didn't happen to her growing up, perhaps? If you seen my mom and I together today we could pass for sisters, that's how much we look alike. There had to be something she experienced with having full lips that she didn't mention. Then just like that the bullying began, I was known for being the little girl in the class with BIG LIPS. It soon became a body part that I greatly disliked in the first grade.

HERE's WHY

The moment I found out that my lips weren't the average size, was the first day of school. Ms. Canlas did an ice breaker so that everyone could introduce themselves. That morning I introduced myself to the class as Aquira Greene. I've always wanted to say my name loud and proud because I believe that I had a very unique name. A few of my classmates laughed from the moment I uttered Aqu—ira out of my mouth, they did not waste any time. As I walked back to my seat I started to hear the whispers and the chuckles saying

"You see her lips? She has some big ass lips."

That was the moment I knew that my lips were bigger than usual. So you mean to tell me that I just introduced myself and that's all they could see? Then I remember one kid in the class say...

"Damn she got some big jumbo lips."

That was my first indication that I was the new joke in the class because of the fullness of my lips. This couldn't be happening I was only in the first grade, six years old to be exact. Could you imagine what was running through my mind at that age? I couldn't process this properly, I wanted to go home that day and cut them off my face. I hoped and prayed that they were smaller so no one would notice how big they were. I wanted them to be so called "normal". This was bugging me out because it was coming from classmates that I would have to see everyday. I didn't want them to make fun of me. From that moment on I knew the school year would possibly be a series of me defending my beauty, or defending myself because I didn't think that having big lips was beauty at the time. I was a tough girl so I would always have a comeback if someone tested me. However, my jokes were considered corny compared to the big lip joke, I was reminded everyday that my lips weren't something that was cool. I would hear things like;

"You have soup cooler lips." Your lips have extra fat on them." "You have pocket lips." "Fish mouth." "Monkey lips."

Blah, blah, blah the list goes on... Looking back at it today as I try to put things in perspective I didn't understand why and who taught these children to make fun of the way that I looked? I couldn't understand why it was even a big deal. Seriously! Later on in life I would come to find out that it was the power of imagery of what these children seen on TV from some of the earliest cartoons, which taught them to hate themselves. Television within itself was a major influence. Children like myself grew up not only hating big lips, they also hated big noses, big butts, nappy hair, darker skin, and big eyes. Having fuller lips was the first insult that came to mind when it came to me, when someone needed a good laugh. It still baffles me to this day when I think about it. I came from a strong family so I was always tough enough to defend myself even if I felt like I wanted to cry. I knew that I just couldn't stay quiet, so I would find something smart to say back to them if they had something mean to say to me. Some days after my homework was done I would study my jokes about whomever I felt like was a constant bully in my class. I used to think long and hard about what to say to make them feel the way I did. I would say things like

"Oh shut up, at least I'm not bald headed."

Back then, there were a lot of perms to make your hair straight and it would make some of the girl's in the school hair fall out. I would say to the boys

"At least I have more hair than your mama."

Even though this wasn't nice I needed to say something that would make them feel less than beautiful just as they made me feel. My hair was really long and beautiful so I thought I had an advantage, some sort of "one up" on them. However, it seemed as though this was going to be a real problem for me moving forward. After my first few weeks of school I got used to it or should I say numb to the jokes. I still felt a bit out of place because as soon as I felt like the kids in my class somehow forgot, I was always reminded that my lips were "too big" and not cool. I've always felt like I wasn't accepted. I remember not wanting to go to school sometimes because I would get teased. It was very frustrating that the physical features I was born with were undesirable to my peers in first grade. I've always felt that I needed to have smaller lips to be beautiful. That pressure alone was devastating. I created this book to talk a little bit about my experiences and to help you along your journey of finding and understanding your own definition of what you call beauty, if you haven't figured this out already.

Don't Let Them Take Your Self Love Away

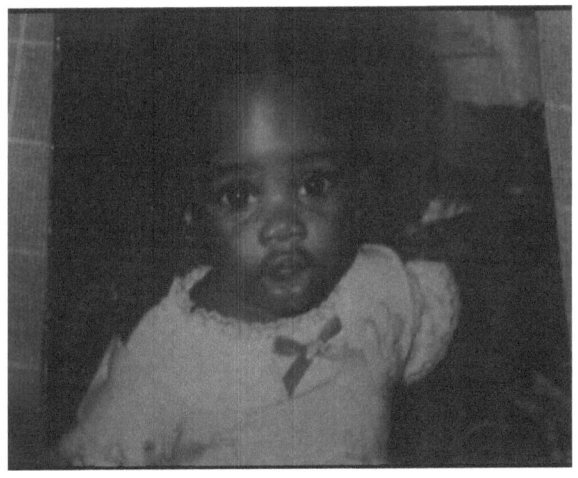

At first they laughed at my beauty in my earlier years of life. I didn't understand why, and as I got older they fell in love with me when I decided to fall in love with me. I went home from school everyday wondering if I did something wrong but I later realized as I got older that they were wrong, not me. They criticized me for being born with some very unique features. If you are reading this book, they probably have done it to you too. I know we can relate on one level or another. I know every single feeling that you've felt. It was hard for me too growing up dealing with these issues. If you are reading this right now your probably in your 20's looking for something promising to read to uplift your spirits about this sudden love for your beauty from society. Guess what? You've picked the right book and this book can only inspire you along your journey if you let it. You may have experienced the same hurt I once did growing up with full lips, fuller than what people called "normal" at the time. What's funny to me is the game has changed, today you don't hear as many jokes as you used to. At some point I had to dig a little deeper inside myself to see that it's not me, it's them. They didn't know true beauty when they saw it. They were taught to discredit themselves and anyone who looked like them or didn't look like them. These teachings began from young ages by outside forces. Sources such as television shows, magazines, and radio stations that all promoted a specific image of beauty and what perfection looked like. The type of images that were shown on these networks back then is what shaped and molded what you think is beauty in today's society. Most days I wanted to go to school & hide my beauty but for some reason I didn't. I showed it off a little more each day. I poked my lips out a little more too. In order for me to have overcome these experiences, little by little, as I got older, I had to show off whatever I was being teased about and say uplifting words to myself in the mirror whenever I felt down. As an adult I still do this. You should try this affirmation and see how it feels...

I am a beautiful woman with lips that people pay a pretty penny for today. I am a goddess. I can and will heal from the discomfort that I felt growing up and any discomfort that I may feel in this very moment. I know for sure that I am powerful. My beauty is authentic. I am bold, brave, and beautiful yesterday, today and tomorrow. I will forever be. Repeat X3

How does that feel? Doesn't it feel powerful? I know after I say it a few times I feel invincible. Saying uplifting words to yourself about yourself sends messages to your subconscious mind and you become stronger day by day. It's like exercising a muscle, the more you work at it the stronger it becomes. At first you may feel a little weird talking to yourself in the mirror but after you start to strengthen your subconscious muscle your confidence will grow and it will be all worth it.

Junior High School

About 6 years later... and still, and still, and still this is a laughing matter. I couldn't believe that after all the bullying in elementary school, it would travel with me to junior high school. I was furious. The jokes were becoming annoying and really just stupid. I couldn't understand why it kept happening. It was like people studied what jokes to say to me, like they took a course on what to say to someone with big lips. Some days it was a constant battle in my head about what it would be like if my lips weren't noticeable. I was always wishing that they could just forget them, but how could they? It was the first thing that stood out when you looked at my face.

I remember one day, I went to class and there was a girl that just maybe had some anger in her or just wanted to pick a fight with me. She said...

"You're in my seat."

"The teacher did not assign seats. I can sit here if I want."

"I never really liked you, you think your cute but you're not with your big ass lips. Now get up out of my seat with your whack ass K-Swiss sneakers."

"Oh well, I'm not getting up and I'm not moving. You can say whatever you want about me. I don't care, get out of my face."

"Your lips are so big you can sweep up the room with them without a broom."

"Whatever, get out of my face before I slap you, you raggedy ass chicken head."

At the time this was the corniest joke ever. Nobody laughed at what I said, instead they laughed at the joke about having big lips. It seemed as though I couldn't get around them. Before she could even say another word I punched her in the face. The whole class went crazy. They started yelling fight, fight, fight in a straight uproar. All I know is that I was on top of her punching and punching, I couldn't stop. After the fight of course I was in big trouble, not only from the teacher and principle, but from my mom. The thought of her having take off work because of me was nerve wrecking. My mother was no joke, she was born and raised in Barbados so being an island girl and going to school in the states was a privilege to her. You know if your parents were from the islands they "didn't play that". She was holding it down as a single parent at the time and taking off from work was not on her agenda. The second I got home I started explaining myself, my mother stopped me dead in my tracks and said

"I don't have time to be taking off work Aquira."

She said it pronounced A-Kee-Ra, in her Barbados accent. Sometimes she called me Kiki for short. She said

"I have bills to pay."

and before I could get another word out she said

"Aquira, you know what? I understand. You had to do what you had to do, to stand up for yourself. Now maybe they will leave you the hell alone."

Honestly it did work, you know the standing up for myself part. Only for a little while though. From that day on, I decided that I don't care about what anyone had to say, I'm not going to let the jokes affect me anymore. Subconsciously I was lying to myself. For some reason I would always seem to think about how big and undesirable they were to everyone at the time. I knew that I would have to set myself free eventually, So I did.

Free Yourself

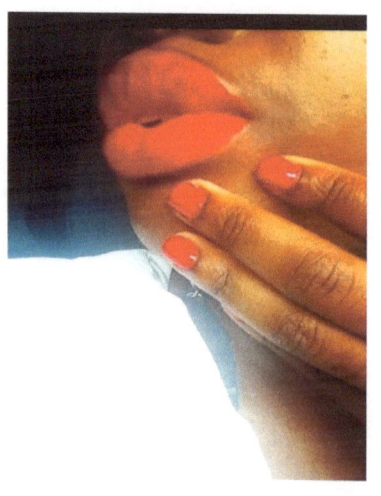

Junior high school was a little different for me, I was older and things were going great. I was in a new school, I even met some new friends. I was so ready to move on from elementary school. Then I came across my first disagreement, and there goes that damn joke again. That's the moment when I felt it, there was something inside of me screaming not again, NOT in freaking junior high school. If I could talk to my younger self, I would say nothing compares to what you have been blessed with. If they can't stop talking about your lips, then that's your super power. Besides, jealousy is love and hate at the same time. In this very moment of reminiscing and writing my words on this paper, I'm taking a deep breath and freeing myself. Freeing myself from the lingering pain that I carried with me from elementary school until now. Now that I know better, I know exactly why women like me were ripped apart for having features that people love and pay thousands of dollars to have today.

My First Kiss, Boys will Be Boys

Then one day out of the blue, for some reason I decided to go to school with lip gloss on. Then all of a sudden the cutest boy in the class finds something interesting about me. It seemed as though before everyone knew I was pretty but they just couldn't get over the fact that I had some big lips and because of it they were uninterested in me.

"Hey Aquira, you look nice today. I like your style, how smart you are, and they way you dress."

"Oh me? Thanks."

"I would love to know how your lips feel, they look so juicy and big. They are really pretty you know?"

"Excuse me? Well that's never going to happen."

"You know you have the sexiest lips in the school, and I know they are probably soft and warm."

"Keep dreaming because I'm not kissing you, besides why would I? I don't even like you like that, and you didn't even notice me until today."

So what you mean to tell me is after all this time, after all this scrutiny your going to change the game and tell me you're actually attracted to my beauty. I wanted to scream but inside I was a little happy, sad to say. I went home with a new attitude. When I think about how I felt after his interest and how good it made me feel I thought about a lot of people in today's society. The majority of the time most people need outside factors to say something good about them before they can see it for themselves, including myself. With my experiences I've learned that everyone will have an opinion and that's none of your business. It ultimately boils down to how you feel about you. When you feel great about yourself others will automatically start to feel that energy you give off and feel the same way about you too.

The very next day I sat in the back of the class because even though I denied the kiss the first time I really wanted him to kiss me. I mean come on, he was one of the cutest freaking boys in the class. I was attracted to him from the first time I laid eyes on him the first day of school. All the girls in the class liked him too. Well, most of them. I didn't care though I knew he would eventually figure out who he liked then make his move. I just didn't think it would be me. I was stuck in between am I pretty like the other girls or are my lips too big?

"Good morning Quira, so did you think about kissing me today?"

"Umm no, absolutely not. I have better things to think about besides, this teacher gives too much damn homework and I'm still sleepy."

"Come on, you know you want to. I'm handsome and I make you laugh. Stop acting like that, come here girl kiss me."

"You better fucking not TOUCH"
….

Before I could get another word out he kissed me. I remember it like it was yesterday. A little moist but not to wet, warm but not to hot. The next day it just seemed like all the boys wanted to engage a little more in conversations with me. That's how I knew he told all his friends that we kissed and what his experience was like.

Let's just say he was love struck after that. Even though I pretended not to want to kiss him, I did. Boys will be boys right? Thinking back about that time and the way boys operated, today it occurs to me that there's never a need to try and figure out who likes you or if you are good enough. The truth of the matter is someone is always looking for exactly what you have to offer.

High School

This is some bullshit! No seriously, you mean to tell me that this big lip joke is just going to haunt me? I thought to myself, when will it stop? The first thing someone sees when they look at me is my lips. Hold up a second, wait a minute! There is something different about these jokes. They're SEXUAL! The jokes were worst than ever. It became a sexual joke to most people and I did not find it funny. People said things like "What that mouth do?" Or "Damn she got some DSL aka dick sucking lips." I was absolutely furious to be associated with those terms because I had fuller lips. It seemed like the older I got, the more attention I was getting because of them. The attention wasn't always a walk in the park. I mean what's a girl to do at that age, I was about 14 or 15 and sucking dick was like taboo to most girls like me. Sex wasn't, but sucking dick was a whole different ball game. When the boys my age talked about oral sex, I thought it was so inappropriate. Every time I turned around It was some inappropriate comment being said. Not to mention the music was encouraging this type of behavior. Well, not in the 90's when music was funky dope fresh. I really love and miss the music back then. Man! I would do anything to bring that type of music back. I started High School in 2002 when music started to take a turn, not as corny as some of the music today in 2016 but taking a slight turn. You still have some musicians today that know how to make a great record like Teyanna Taylor and J Cole. Anyway, at this age I was completely into boys, but not as fast as most girls I knew. I was into one or two boys which was cool but you should have seen some of the other girls, they were into multiple guys at a time and trying new things without hesitation. How else did boys even know what a pair of lips felt like on their private parts so young? I remember hearing stories of girls in staircases giving head like it was nothing. One girl was so opened with it she went around telling her story or her story somehow got out. Even though by the time it got around to me it probably wasn't the full story anyway. Here's what I heard happened...

"She was jerking his dick with her hand for a while but then got bored with it because it was so junior high school. High school was just different so she wanted to get more close with him. She just had to suck his dick just to be able to tell her friends that she did it! She closed her eyes and he was moaning so she kept moving. She even mentioned that she had tasted his pre-cum and everything that was dripping out of the tip of it. Then she went on to say she got a little tired and just focused on the softer part. He screamed her name, then she felt hot cum hit the roof of her mouth! She said she couldn't get away from him before all of his cum poured into her mouth."

This was just too much, very intriguing but way too much for me at the age of fourteen. I guess that was around the time when every single teenage guy in America got this bright idea that when you see a girl with big lips, it means she must suck dick. I'm just saying how in the hell else did this myth come about? It was always hell having to correct someone who associated me with dick sucking because my lips were big. I would respond to them and say things like "Sorry dumb ass I don't suck dick." It seriously was like trying to convince your eighteen-year-old high school kid to believe in Santa. It was pretty much a headache but again everyone thought it was funny. Time after time again I wished that my lips weren't noticeable because every guy I came across was talking about "Damn look at her lips" or "You see them lips?", "You know what that means." I would always respond or think to myself "Shut the fuck up you idiotic punk, that's not what that means. I have big lips because I was born with it not because I'm great at sucking dick."

My Lip Pout Brings All The Boys To The Yard

Look at that face. How can I not love it? I'm talking to all women with the sexiest lips on the planet. Hey you, yes you. At least this is what I had to tell myself after of all these years of confusion of what beauty really was. Here's a little secret that I learned over the years. Your beauty is naturally yours whatever that may be and to the women with fuller lips, just know you were born that way. You have no liquid injected into them to make them bigger. No make-up kits, lip enhancers, nothing at all. This is all you, this is your authentic self. Remember to hold your head high with pride and dignity because one day you will realize all along you had the juice. People today believe it's one the most desirable features to have, and even if they didn't all that matters is that you believe that your beautiful. I honestly feel that people all over the world for decades already seen beauty in you. They just didn't want you to realize it because a person of your culture had it. It has become some form of sex symbol today. I mean women everywhere are doing duck lips and trying all kinds of lip enhancers. Around my college days if you had full lips all the guys would just strike a conversation with you just to see them move. It seemed as though the tables have turned. People were beginning to change their mind about how they felt about fuller lips. It was no longer funny or unattractive to everyone. However, no one has the power to flip your switch. The switch to make you feel good about you, belongs to you. You have control of that switch. You can turn it off or you can turn it on. You can turn it to love or you can turn it to hate. So keep pouting those beautiful lips. Keep showing them off. Blessings to you, you beautiful Queen.

The Love of Men

It's amazing how much love I got from real men, conscious men. The love that I was receiving from some men was exhilarating. As I grew older men from all over the world started to become in love with my features, if they weren't already. I guess it was the way they looked or the way they felt when kissed or touched. Fuller lips are naturally kissable, lovable, and pleasurable. I can't begin to tell you how many times men compliment me about them on a daily basis. If I got paid for every time I was stopped in the street about my lips,

I would probably be wealthy by now. Sometimes they would come up to me and say things like, "Hey, can I tell you something?" I would respond and say, "Sure, tell me what?" Then they would proceed to say, "Did you know you have the most beautiful lips in the world?" Men and women would come up to me and say so many great things about my lips. One time this man came up to me and said "Damn if you were mine, I would just walk up to you grab your face and gently kiss you passionately every chance I get". Things like this would always make me blush but it also would get me thinking. Hmmm... not bad coming from a place of feeling discomfort before. The fuller lips that women like me have are now an attractive feature that women from other ethnic backgrounds often attempt to duplicate all the time. For some strange reason they get praised for it and women like myself don't. We get over looked and under valued like we weren't the ones born with it. It's such a damn shame. I guess it was because of all the bad experiences I've been through in the past that made my mind wonder. It was like my lips became a sudden gift and not a curse. If you ask me, it shouldn't have been this way at all.

Having the full lips that I have isn't half the reason why men love women like myself. It is actually in addition to what we already have that you can't buy. The main thing they were attracted to is the fact that

I come with a brain. Having some intellect can go very far, it doesn't really pay to be an air head. Sometimes I would speak to my male friends and get their opinions on why they loved women with fuller lips. Almost all of them, deeply expressed the fact that on top of a woman having fuller lips and other features like a curvy body or big butt, they were really much more intrigued by an independent, hardworking, influential women. Ask any man with a great head on his shoulders. It simply makes them love and connect with you even more on a higher level. Especially when you have more than beauty to bring to the table. Most of my home boys expressed that women like myself are definitely one of a kind, and when you get one with the right mindset you must hold on to them. When a woman can embody these qualities and strive for success there's nothing more attractive. What else can be sexier than that? Men all across the world just love women who are focused and motivated to make something of themselves. Some believe that these qualities are something that only a rare breed of women have. It is a real game changer when you just give off a sense of flavor, classiness, and most of all confidence. The love of men, mainly our men was music to my ears. To know that I was loved, cherished and desired helped me to take pride in my unique features but it didn't change what I needed to learn about myself. Self love is the best love. The love of men was always secondary to what I needed to feel from myself first.

However, I can't lie it sent chills down my spine and reminded me that only a king can love a queen, but he must first be conscious enough to know that he is a king. Having fuller lips came from a culture that is so rich and so deeply rooted. The essence of me just being a woman of melanin, turned me on. It made me so proud of who I am and who I've always been. When you have a culture that is frowned upon but is always the natural source of everything beautiful you have a different perspective about your beauty once you learn the history of it. The moment you find out everywhere you go you will light up a room. Today I can stand strong and say there is nothing like the love from a king. Now that we are on the topic, my proudest moments are seeing how powerful a woman becomes when that magnetic energy of a king join forces with her, that is one hell of a sight to see.

The Portrait

Your beauty can speak volumes, if you let it. I had to understand that I bring something very different to the table, and that was authenticity. Society can't discredit me for my beauty then turn around and pay for it. It's kind of crazy when your features are seen on someone of another ethnic group, then they call it trendy and beautiful. Big lips aren't anything new, whether they're natural, surgically injected or a product of some awesome makeup skills. I went from being so insecure about them to cutting all my hair off so you can see them better. Okay, that wasn't the reason I cut my hair but seriously you never know how beautiful you can be by just changing your mindset towards what your insecure about. You should always no matter what be strong, be fearless, but most importantly be you. If you don't society will chew you up and spit you out.

The Disrespect of Men

Time: 1:34pm

Date: 10/10/2015

Scene: Somewhere in the boogie down Bronx.

Disrespectful Man: Hey Ma, how are you?

Me: Hi, I'm fine and yourself?

Disrespectful Man: Can I ask you what kind of dog that is?

Me: A Shih Tzu

Disrespectful Man: Can I have your number to get to know you better?

Me: Oh, no thank you. I'm really not interested in getting to know anyone at the moment.

Disrespectful Man:

What? Don't act like you don't want to suck my dick with your big ass lips.

What you think you have those lips for? (Turns his head to his friend in the passenger side of the car and says loudly) She got them big ass lips and don't want to give me her number, so I can get to know her and she can suck my dick. Damn she got some big ass lips. (Turns back to me and I'm stuck I can't even move, I'm in a state of shock) BITCH stop acting like you too good to suck my dick.

Me: Blank stares...

    There were so many words that I was thinking but nothing came out. It felt something like a dream, and your having a fight but can't hit your opponent. It was like your running from Freddy Kruger in your sleep and you can't get away until you wake up. My mind was cloudy. I snapped out of it after I heard a few cars beeping for the guy to move. "What a freaking ignorant asshole", I thought to myself. That day had to be the most embarrassing day of my life. I felt real pain in this moment because it was disgustingly disrespectful. To top it off I couldn't believe this idiot was holding up traffic just to disrespect me. Such a horrific two minutes of my life. When all the cars passed, I waited for the next light. I ran upstairs to tell my boyfriend then ten minutes later I called my mom and told her. My boyfriend was pissed off. He really didn't tolerate disrespect.

However, he was calmer than I was, he has always been a calm guy from the time that I met him. That's just his human nature. He said "People are mentally ill and you can't take it personal but if I were there I would have beat his ass." My mom was like "What the fuck? He said what to you? People are just so stupid and ignorant." My mom was always ready to aim, shoot and fire. She's a riot when it comes to her daughters. I sat down on my bed and thought to myself. Out of all the incidents that I've ever experienced this was one of the ones that I wasn't only thinking about myself when it happened. All I could think about was, how many young girls or women have to live through this everyday. Why is it that having full lips are always associated with sucking dick? How many women are going through this very same thing right now? Something must be done, said or addressed. So I started to write, I didn't know my thoughts would turn into a brief book about my lips. Which makes me laugh as I write this because what I know for sure is that your thoughts become things. Not very long ago I was thinking about this book and the success it would have in helping women like me and I project that it will be a New York Times best seller.

Boost No Yesus!

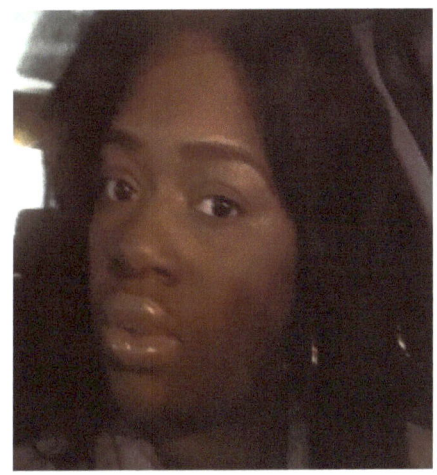

My lips have honestly helped boost my confidence in my adult life. Mostly because some people obsessed over them. I mean, they drooled over them like they were a piece of steak from their favorite steak house cooked to perfection. When ever I felt the urge of an ego trip I would gloss them up and take a walk, go to the supermarket, or upload a photo to my social media. It was cool to see how many people was obsessing over them after all the years of hate. The compliments worked for me every time. However, it didn't matter whether they were glossed up or not. People were like vultures and they held no punches. I can't lie in one of my adult relationships it would almost amaze me how deeply he got weak after an episode of a BJ. It was sort of like something came over him each time. A total 180 completely different from his normal self, the way he moaned and said things to me. It made me feel like a sensual goddess.

It was the way I could make a masculine man transform into a child like state and behave like a lost puppy. It tickled me inside to see how he would act, like he was depressed, moping around when he didn't receive any or I wasn't in the mood. I can't lie it was interesting how I would be reminded how good it felt to him just to have the fullness of my lips touch his most sensitive spot. He would say things like "Damn baby can't nobody do what you do with those lips you have", or "I would rather have your full lips over smaller ones any day", or "I can't live without them pretty sexy ass lips" and so on. Every night before bed he would beg for it, it was like he needed it to sleep through the night or something. Some nights he really just couldn't fall sleep without it. It was like a drug. I guess it was because of the way I treated it. The way I would use my whole mouth and emphasize the movements of my lips, how I could get completely into it like suggested in this book I read called the Power of Now by Eckhart Tolle. He spoke about being completely engaged in the moment without a single thought or distraction and focus on the task at hand until it is complete. Don't get it misconstrued I am no expert or super head kind of girl. I haven't been around the block but the very few that had the key to unlock that door was in for a treat. I just knew I was in control every time and it was definitely a boost for me no Yesus!

Another confidence boost was just waking up and simply putting on lipstick to go outside and run errands. The different colors were exciting, especially the ones that make my lips pop. Sometimes the colors that I choose are so bright and beautiful that people just would stare in amazement. Some people would stare like I shouldn't have it on or whatever, but that was their problem not mine. I guess it was because my lips already stood out. I didn't care because the fact that they were staring already let me know I stood out from the rest. This would always make my day because I knew that I had left a lasting impression on whom ever I crossed paths with.

You just have to know that you are POWERFUL. Once you discover it, you will then become more confident to not care what anyone thinks of you. Even if the skin you're in and the features that you have might get over looked or even dissed the majority of the time. You have to be bold enough to tell yourself you are the most beautiful creature that ever walked this planet earth or mars, Lol. I didn't learn this until I got a little bit older. In a billion-dollar industry of plastic surgery and cosmetic care that can change the way your lips look, you better be brave and bold enough to say I was born with it: No Injections Needed. Be brave enough to stand up for yourself when there are critics. Sometimes the best way to respond is to say nothing at all. What I have learned through experience is that people love to place you in a box or category. They love to tell you that you can't do this or you can't be that. What I know for sure, which is a phrase that I read from an Oprah book called "What I know for sure" is, you are you. You can be whatever is it that you want to be, do whatever you want to do. If there is no lane for it, then create it. Find your authentic you and embody that. Be bold enough to make mistakes and pick yourself up when you fall, no matter how many times you do so. In life it's not about how hard you can hit, it's about how hard you can get hit and how quick you pick yourself back up.

Society, Thank You

Thank you to all the hashtag lip challenges on social media that says having fuller lips is now trendy, with no credit given to the ones who were born with it. What should be said is all hail to the women who were teased and picked on, your features are to die for. Hashtag that. It is disgusting to recognize now that fuller lips are beautiful. Don't make believe that this is a new trend. It is very disrespectful to the people that were ridiculed and made fun of and told that they weren't beautiful because they had big lips. Think about all the little girls your hurt. The ones that went home from school wishing they could just rip their lips off. I'm talking to you society, sometimes you can be so backwards. I'm not talking to everyone but for those who are now calling this a trend, this is for you. It's funny how it's acceptable to have some of our features or characteristics but not too many. Having voluptuous lips is not a trend it is in fact something that has been around since women like me were born Millenniums ago. It has just been overlooked time after time again until someone of another ethnic back ground goes and pays for it. Seriously, do your research old comics have always degraded people like me, and our lips were always comically huge in the old cartoons. It's a shame what we have been taught through imagery and propaganda of what "real beauty" is. Rarely women like me are EVER praised for our own natural features.

Some women aren't known to have fuller lips and they have to depend on lip plumper's and lipsticks. Some go as far as lip injections to get a full set of luscious lips. Our lips are so in right now which pissed me off because it should have been in from the very beginning. Honestly, it shouldn't be superior to other shapes or sizes. In today's world most lip sticks and lip glosses seem to have lip plumping formulas. It's very clear that we have gorgeous, seductive lips that cost a pretty penny for women with thinner lips to obtain. What I don't understand is why would you want to be someone else? I've seen so many drop dead beautiful women with thinner lips who have other features to die for as well. Everyone has their own preference of what they like but to each it's own. Coming from a place of ridicule I've always needed to dig deeper and find that beautiful goddess inside of me to say you know what? My lips are and forever will be incredibly, breathtakingly stunning. Period.

A Note To Future Self

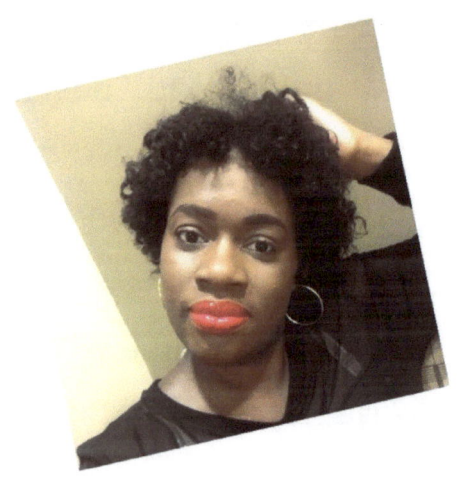

I would have never thought the day I walked in my first grade class all the way up until today that I would be writing a book for young adults and women who are just like myself. You may have already experienced some challenges or maybe still going through some of the same issues. I am a young woman who just decided to go for it no matter if I failed. I am not afraid to do and say what's on my heart. When I first started to write this book, it honestly came to me in a dream after seeing the most recent ridiculous lip challenge on social media. It also came after my most recent incident when I was disrespected for just having full lips and walking down the street. I decided I should write about it but I didn't really take it seriously until something came over me to start writing. I knew by doing so I could help someone else and my future self will thank me for it later on in life. You see since I was a little girl I've always wanted to be an actress. I've always wanted to leave an impact in this world. Leaving my mark is so important to me. Never did it occur to me that it will stem from a book, that would open up opportunities for me to live my dreams. Although along my journey I've came across so many distractions, it would never stop me from going after what I believe in. Today I have everything I could have ever asked for. A heart of gold and a peaceful spirit with an amazing acting career. I am front row at the Oscars and the Golden Globes, with consecutive wins. I'm getting hired and co-creating roles that I couldn't imagine, in a million years, getting or even existing. I have a beautiful family, with a wonderful husband and great friends to share all of my success with.

I'm endorsing multiple brands, including my own that applies to my principles and what I believe in. I now have a lipstick line, multiple fragrances, clothing lines, books, movies and television shows, you name it I have it all. Everything I touch turns into gold. For some reason I always knew that my destiny would find me. I always had faith that I would make it very far and leave a legacy for my family. I've always had the courage and determination, even if I failed. Being driven was just a characteristic that I have embodied over the years. Today I can honestly say I'm living the dream.

Dear future self see you soon,

Aquira Greene

Now its your turn, do yourself a favor and write a short brief paragraph to your future self. It doesn't have to be extensive, even that will grow as you grow.

Please email me your paragraphs. I am going to use the best ones for an upcoming project.

Visit www.aquiragreene.com

Instagram @Aquira.Greene

God, Family, Empire.

www.ingramcontent.com/pod-product-compliance
Lightning Source LLC
Chambersburg PA
CBHW040458240426
43665CB00039B/80